RELIGIONS OF THE WORLD

I Am

Jewish

❖ BERNARD P. WEISS ❖

The Rosen Publishing Group's

PowerKids Press

New York

W

Published in 1996 by The Rosen Publishing Group, Inc.
29 East 21st Street, New York, NY 10010

First Edition

Photo credits: Cover photo © Bill Aron; p. 4 © Bobbe Wolf/International Stock; p. 7, 16, 19 © Bill Aron; p. 8 © V. Shone/Gamma Liaison; p. 11 © George Ancona/International Stock; pp. 12, 15 courtesy of the Dizengoff family; p. 20 © E. Baitel/Gamma Liaison.

Book Design and Layout: Erin McKenna and Kim Sonsky

Weiss, Bernard P.
    I am Jewish / Bernard P. Weiss.
        p.   cm.—(Religions of the world)
    Includes index.
    Summary: Introduces the ancient religion of Judaism through the eyes of a Jewish child living in St. Louis.
    ISBN 0-8239-2349-5
    1. Judaism—juvenile literature. [l. Judaism.] I. Title. II. Series: Religions of the world (Rosen Publishing Group)
BM573.W45 1996
296—dc20   96-733
                                              CIP
                                        AC r96

Manufactured in the United States of America

Contents

Being Jewish

My name is David. I live in St. Louis. I am Jewish. I have two sisters named Rebecca and Sarah.

The very first Jew was named Abraham. Abraham lived more than four thousand years ago. Jews believe that Abraham promised God that he and his family would obey God's laws.

Jewish law is an important part of being Jewish. The Ten Commandments are part of Jewish law. There are many other Jewish laws that tell how Jewish people should behave.

◄ *As in all religions, Jewish people follow the laws of their faith.*

The Sabbath

Keeping the Sabbath is one of the Ten Commandments. The Sabbath begins every Friday at sundown. It ends after sundown on Saturday. The Sabbath is our most holy day.

The Sabbath celebrates the seventh day of Creation. That is the day God rested after making the world. That is why we do not work on the Sabbath. We prepare food for all of our Sabbath meals before Sabbath begins. This is so that we will not have to cook on the Sabbath.

The celebration of Sabbath begins with the lighting of the Sabbath candles. ▶

Synagogue

On the Sabbath, my family says special prayers. We go to **synagogue** (SIN-a-gog), too. Synagogue is another word for temple, or house of prayer. When my father prays, he wears a **talit** (ta-LEET), or prayer shawl. We also cover our heads with small caps called **yarmulkes** (YAH-mah-kahs).

A **rabbi** (RAB-bye) leads the Sabbath service with the help of a cantor. The rabbi is a religious guide and teacher and helps us solve problems in life. The cantor chants traditional Jewish songs and prayers.

◀ *A synagogue is a Jewish house of prayer and worship.*

The Hebrew Bible

At the synagogue, the rabbi reads from the **Torah** (TOR-rah). Torah is the Hebrew name for the first five books of the Hebrew Bible. You might know the Hebrew Bible as the Old Testament. The Torah was written long, long ago in Hebrew, the language of the Jews. The Torah talks about Jewish history, Jewish law, and Jewish belief.

In Hebrew, my name looks like this:

דֶּסֶד

I can't read it yet, but I will learn when I am older.

The Torah is so special that no one is allowed to touch it. ▶

Bar Mitzvah

When I turn thirteen, I will have a **Bar Mitzvah** (bar MITZ-vah) ceremony. Bar Mitzvah is an old ritual. Before my Bar Mitzvah, I will learn to read and speak Hebrew. I will read from the Torah in front of everyone in the synagogue. This shows that I am an adult, ready to share the responsibilities of Jewish life. Then we will have a big party to celebrate.

When my sister Sarah turns twelve, she will have a **Bat Mitzvah** (bot MITZ-vah).

◀ *Once a boy has had his Bar Mitzvah, he is considered an adult.*

Marriage

My sister Rebecca is getting married soon. My father says that marriage is one of the most **sacred** (SAY-kred) events in Jewish life because it is a new beginning for the bride and groom. They will be married under a wedding canopy called a **chupah** (HUP-pah). Our rabbi will perform the wedding. At the end of the ceremony, the groom will break a glass by stepping on it, and everyone will shout *"Mazel tov!"* which means congratulations. Then we will celebrate with a big party.

In a Jewish wedding, the bride and groom are married under a chupah. ▶

The High Holy Days

Rosh Hashanah is the Jewish New Year. It occurs every fall. Nine days after Rosh Hashanah, we celebrate Yom Kippur. Rosh Hashanah and Yom Kippur are very holy days. We call them the High Holy Days. During the High Holy Days, we stop and think about what we did wrong in the last year. We ask God to forgive us. To show God that we are sorry for what we have done, we fast on Yom Kippur. That means that we don't eat or drink anything.

◀ *To indicate the beginning and end of the High Holy Days, the rabbi blows a special horn called a shofar.*

Passover

My favorite holiday is Passover. My family and our friends get together for a big meal called a **seder** (SAY-dur). Before Passover, we clean our house and remove all the bread. This is to remind us that when the Jews fled Egypt, they didn't have time to bake bread.

At the seder, we read from the **Haggadah** (huh-GOD-dah), which tells the story of how the Jews left Egypt. We remember how God freed the Jews from slavery. We remember Moses, and how he led them out of Egypt. We sing special songs, eat special foods, and say prayers to celebrate our freedom.

The Haggadah is a special book ▶
that is used only during Passover.

Jerusalem

I live in the United States, but many Jews live in Israel. Israel is a country in the Middle East. In Israel, many people speak Hebrew.

Jerusalem is the most holy city in Israel. It was the city in which the First Temple was built. That Temple was destroyed in one of many wars in Jerusalem, and a Second Temple was built. If you go to Jerusalem today, you can still see a wall from the Second Temple. It is called the Western, or Wailing, Wall. Many Jews go there to pray. I hope to go to Jerusalem to pray at the Wailing Wall some day.

◀ *Jews from all over the world go to the Wailing Wall in Jerusalem to pray.*

Chanukah

Chanukah celebrates a **miracle** (MEER-a-kul) that happened thousands of years ago.

According to tradition, a sacred lamp always had to be burning in the Temple. Once the Jews were fighting their enemies in Jerusalem. When they won back the Temple, they had only enough oil in the Temple lamp for one night. But miraculously, the lamp burned for eight days. It was just long enough for them to get more oil!

Each night of Chanukah, we light the **menorah** (meh-NOR-ah) and exchange presents.

Glossary

Bar/Bat Mitzvah (bar/bot MITZ-vah) Celebration of a Jewish youth becoming an adult.

chupah (HUP-pah) Wedding canopy.

Haggadah (huh-GOD-dah) Book that tells the story of the Jews leaving Egypt.

menorah (meh-NOR-ah) A candle holder used in Jewish worship.

miracle (MEER-a-kul) Something wonderful that doesn't normally happen.

rabbi (RAB-bye) Religious guide and teacher.

sacred (SAY-kred) Holy.

seder (SAY-dur) Passover celebration.

synagogue (SIN-a-gog) Temple; house of prayer.

talit (ta-LEET) Prayer shawl.

Torah (TOR-rah) First five books of the Hebrew Bible.

yarmulke (YAH-mah-kah) Head covering.

Index